CO

Bysing Wood Primary School, Faversham

Ashleigh A E Badejo (8)	1
Eli Eastmond-Jones (7)	2
Evie Smith (8)	3
Lyla Ogden (7)	4
Lilia Kostadinova (7)	5
Sarah-Jane Rossiter (7)	6
Leo Parsons (8)	7
Ruby Richards (7)	8
Luke Davis (7)	9
Myla Leach (8)	10
Tyler Powell (7)	11
Harry McCullough-Kerwick (7)	12
Tyler Jolly (7)	13
Hayden Pilbeam (8)	14
Phoebe Whiskin (7)	15
Bobby Blake (8)	16
Dylan Morris (8)	17
Holly Barker (7)	18
Hadrian Bharke (8)	19
Effie-Anne Dean (7)	20

Fox Hill Primary School, Sheffield

Daniel Minani (9)	21
Aiden Gowler (8)	22
Tanishka Harshan (10)	23
Alice Blanksby (9)	24
Phoebe Poulton (11) & Katie-Jo Myers	25
Trisha Eboigbe (9)	26
Ranae Abbott (10)	28
Amin Omer (11)	29
Luke Manning (9)	30

Alfie Walker (10)	31
Olivia Naylor (8)	32
Nathan Taylor (8)	33
Sonia Hussain (7)	34
Sienna Gibbon (9)	35

John Rankin Junior School, Newbury

Alessia Cattanach (8)	36
Bella Collins (10)	38
Dominika Racz (10)	40
Bhuvi Deegwal (10)	41
Harrow (9)	42
Lily Johnson (10)	44
Lily Everett (8)	45
Phoebe Avarne (9)	46
Edith Powell (9)	47
Imogen Lewis (10)	48
Neysa Amoah (10)	49
Evelynn Wallace (9)	50
Emily Stott (10)	51
Reuben Fairless (8)	52
Phoebe Davies (10)	53
Chloe Kaburu (8)	54
Josh Brooks (9)	55
Mya Polehampton (8)	56
Shanaya Gowda (8)	57
Elise Horridge (8)	58
Arabella Breakspear (10)	59
Erin Austin (8)	60
Aaria Pike (9)	61
Oscar Ruddock (9)	62
Hannah Goldschmidt (10)	63
Hari Sarajini-Hodge (10)	64
Zain Hussain (9)	65

Grace Hart (10)	66
Stan Bull (9)	67
Nilesh Sharma (10)	68
Edie Osborne (9)	69
Rose Creasey (9)	70
Aoife Robertson (8)	71
Fifi Douglas (9)	72
Esme Appleton (9)	73
Amelia Caplin-Bird (10)	74
Sally Kutesa (8)	75
Eve Wheeler (9)	76

Kensington Avenue Primary School, Thornton Heath

Vivaan Bakku (8)	77
Laila Sewell-Green (9)	78
Kaira Tailor (10)	80
Miguel Kusi (10)	81
Skylar Madden (8)	82
Esha Tailor (9)	83
Nyle Rafiq (9)	84
Alvita Justice Ndidi (9)	85
Aymen Joudari (10)	86
Gracie Cook Wright (8)	87
Samim K (9)	88
Azraa Roy (8)	89
Livia Silva Castro (9)	90
Eesa Choudhry (9)	91
Zahra Kellman (9)	92
Nita Surafel (8)	93
Nur Khan (9)	94
Faith Williams-Flemming (8)	95
Misri Patel (9)	96
Mouna Bovell Nai (9)	97
Makiba Amanuel (8)	98
Kelly Wallace (9)	99

Llandrillo Yn Rhos Primary School, Rhos On Sea

Dima Mandziuk (11)	100
Ada Williams (10)	102
Georgina Hagley (10)	103
Hana Carroll (10)	104
Ambar Sureya Jones (10)	105
Daisy Temple (7)	106
Madison Temple (9)	107
Grace Bowden (10)	108
Seren Evans (11)	109
Georgie Naylor (8)	110
Ophelia McGuffie (8)	111
Caitlin Dean (8)	112
Reece Gallagher (9)	113
L Jones (9)	114

Milwards Primary School & Nursery, Harlow

Jayden Corbett (8)	115
Harrison Blayney (7)	116
Noah Lewis (8)	118
Areesha Qasim (8)	119
Samirah Nasreen (8)	120
Micah March (7)	121
Ella Findon (8)	122
Vyara T (7)	123
Abigail Dockerill (8)	124
Kajetan Woloch (7)	125
Amelia Taylor Cook (7)	126
Zachary William (7)	127
Evie Yeomans (8)	128
Riley Chingwara (7)	129
Noah Thompson (7)	130
Lily Turkoglu (8)	131
Elsie Thomas (8)	132
Olivia Fick (8)	133
Frankie Lee (7)	134
Oliver Sutton (7)	135

Verses From The UK

Edited By Lynsey Evans

First published in Great Britain in 2024 by:

Young Writers
Remus House
Coltsfoot Drive
Peterborough
PE2 9BF
Telephone: 01733 890066
Website: www.youngwriters.co.uk

FOREWORD

Welcome Reader, to a world of dreams.

For Young Writers' latest competition, we asked our writers to dig deep into their imagination and create a poem that paints a picture of what they dream of, whether it's a make-believe world full of wonder or their aspirations for the future.

The result is this collection of fantastic poetic verse that covers a whole host of different topics. Let your mind fly away with the fairies to explore the sweet joy of candy lands, join in with a game of fantasy football, or you may even catch a glimpse of a unicorn or another mythical creature. Beware though, because even dreamland has dark corners, so you may turn a page and walk into a nightmare!

Whereas the majority of our writers chose to stick to a free verse style, others gave themselves the challenge of other techniques such as acrostics and rhyming couplets.

Each piece in this collection shows the writers' dedication and imagination – we truly believe that seeing their work in print gives them a well-deserved boost of pride, and inspires them to keep writing, so we hope to see more of their work in the future!

THE POEMS

Knights And Dragons

As I lay in my comfy warm bed,
I arrived in a wonderful dream,
A realm of dragons, fierce and bold,
I could see some with scales of silver, iron and gold,
Their fiery breath ignited the sky.

As knights in armour,
Brave and high, ride forth to battle,
Swords in hand,
Against the beasts that rule the land.

The sky was as red as flames,
Giant volcanoes erupting,
The grass and flowers fading in the strange wind,
And the roar of the thunder in the air.

Then I woke with a scare,
Relieved to find myself at home,
I could hear loud thunder outside,
But I still fell back to sleep calmly.

Ashleigh A E Badejo (8)
Bysing Wood Primary School, Faversham

Lights Out And Away We Go!

Once upon a dream,
I arrived in New Mexico with Evie.
I was getting ready for a race.

Tall mountains everywhere
On the beach, there were crabs snapping
The sand was so hot,
It burnt my feet!

Stomping out in the distance,
Was a huge, gigantic dragon,
Roaring in the abyss and finally
We arrived.

Here ladies and gentlemen,
We're in the Mexican circuit
With fourteen corners.

Lights out and away we go
Lewis gets a great start
Eli's in second place
Who is going to win the race?

Eli Eastmond-Jones (7)
Bysing Wood Primary School, Faversham

The Phenomenal Dream

A long time ago,
When I was snuggled in bed,
I dreamt a phenomenal dream,
Where I saw something ruby red,
Upon a spotty mushroom.

When I opened my eyes,
I saw the sun wave,
As I heard mythical creatures roar,
The loudest of them all was Dynamite!
When a cute, baby goblin made a law.

As I was going to a cave,
With dragons and monsters,
I felt very brave,
I felt a bit calm, I guess.

As I stepped in,
I heard a noise like fireworks popping,
It was a fight about delicious bananas.

Evie Smith (8)
Bysing Wood Primary School, Faversham

Experiencing Dreamland

Once upon a dream,
I was all cosy in bed,
When a strange mythical land formed in my head,

There were dancing ballerinas doing ballet all around
me,
With the clouds like candyfloss,
Suddenly a unicorn with wings,
Picked me up and...

Whizzing through the air we soared,
I was a bit confused,
But also a bit amazed at the same time,
When I got down,
I danced to my favourite song,

Although it was lovely there,
I was all on my own,
My mum shook me gently,
Then I was home.

Lyla Ogden (7)
Bysing Wood Primary School, Faversham

Star Stickers

I fell asleep and had a dream
I saw a massive world
With star stickers shining in the sky.

One sticker came flying by
And stuck on my cheek, like a superhero!

I turned into a superhero! With a
Star sticker, super goggles, super
Helmet and super roller skates.

On my whizzy roller skates
I flew through fluffy clouds
Whoosh, crash! What was that?
I started to spin around
And caught a shooting star
Down I went to Earth.

I woke up in my bed
With my shooting star.

Lilia Kostadinova (7)
Bysing Wood Primary School, Faversham

Polar Express Train

I stepped into a world of dreams
When I came outside, I saw a flash
And it burnt my eyes
It was a massive train.

I heard a shout, "All aboard!"
Running, I hopped onto the train
Just as it started to rain.

Whoosh, sped the train along the tracks
The train went *choo, choo!*
As it sped through the snow
On its way to the North Pole.

I stepped outside into the deep snow
And saw Santa on his sleigh
I jumped in excitement
And saw the train smile.

Sarah-Jane Rossiter (7)
Bysing Wood Primary School, Faversham

The Factory

Last night I had a dream,
A big brown door stood in front of me.
I opened the door, and what did I see?
Willy Wonka's Chocolate Factory.

I saw a chocolate lake,
That looked really yummy.
So I asked Wonka if I could have a sip,
To fill up my tummy.

He replied, "Yes, if you have a golden ticket."
Luckily I found one in my trouser pocket.
He asked, "Would you like to meet the Oompa
Loompas?"
I said, "Yes."
"Don't get lost," he called.

Leo Parsons (8)
Bysing Wood Primary School, Faversham

Magical Creature

I was all cosy in my bed
When I entered the world of dreams in my head.

I was in a forest of fairy-tale green
When I heard *twit-twoo* - a baby owl was near me.

I heard a crack! Then felt a *thud*
It filled me with dreams
A coconut had fallen onto my head.

A beautiful parrot flew by with its rainbow wings
It looked at me
And began to sing.

It sang, "I know you find this land cool,
But now you have to wake up for school!"

Ruby Richards (7)
Bysing Wood Primary School, Faversham

Untitled

Once upon a dream, I woke up in a strange land,
In the distance, I could see a giant castle.
I heard a loud roar!
It made me jump and shriek,
A white cyclops appeared in a fire as hot as flames.
I ran like the wind towards the castle
The moon shone like a lightbulb
Strong armour and a sword appeared made of ice.
I headed back towards the fiery cyclops
I jumped on his back
My ice sword smouldered as I used it to defeat him.

Luke Davis (7)
Bysing Wood Primary School, Faversham

Nightmares

N ightmares form into my dream,
I see things that make me want to scream,
G etting worse and worse every night,
"H elp!" I shout with such a fright,
T imes where they think I lie, it's true!
M any don't know how much I've been through,
A nother after another,
R estarting every day,
E very night, I cry,
S cary stars shine in my eyes.

Myla Leach (8)
Bysing Wood Primary School, Faversham

Roller Coaster

Last night I had a dream
As I fell asleep in my bed
I found myself at a roller coaster park

There were roller coasters all around
Going up and down
Making lots of sounds

I got on a roller coaster that was as red as fire
Slowly like a sloth, we went up, then whooshed down
As fast as a cheetah

Tyler, Tyler, Tyler! It is time for school!
Goodbye roller coaster park
See you again tonight!

Tyler Powell (7)
Bysing Wood Primary School, Faversham

The Venomous Spider

I dreamed a dream in bed
And found myself in a busy city
I didn't hear the venomous spider
As he crawled out of the drain.

I heard a *crash!*
He'd jumped on three cars
As big as Bigfoot and black like ink
His smooth body ran towards me.

Thunder roared and it started to rain
I saw his sharp fangs
He flew towards me
I woke up, cosy in bed
Hearing rain on my window.

Harry McCullough-Kerwick (7)
Bysing Wood Primary School, Faversham

The Magic Universe

Last night, I had a dream
I found myself in an odd world
I saw a massive dragon

There was candy everywhere
The trees were lollipops
With footballs hanging down.

I heard the dragon was like lightning
It was as long as a python
And as red as fire

I woke up with a jump
My sister was in my room
Tickling me so I woke up!

Tyler Jolly (7)
Bysing Wood Primary School, Faversham

An Indian Adventure

I dreamed a dream in bed
Then I found myself in India
Getting ready for an adventure.

The bright sun looked down at me
With fluffy clouds above me
The empty plains stretched for miles.

I saw a scary dragon in the distance
Roaring like a lion.
As it winked at me, I laughed
I heard my brother's voice
And woke up safe in bed.

Hayden Pilbeam (8)
Bysing Wood Primary School, Faversham

Waves

I dream a dream in bed, feeling lazy
The big waves crash in the stormy seas
The small waves dance near the happy shore.

The waves are as calm as a sleeping bunny.

The white seagulls are screeching for food.

The crabs walk slowly on the sandy beach.

The sun is peeking through the fluffy clouds.
I feel happy and sad.

Phoebe Whiskin (7)
Bysing Wood Primary School, Faversham

Dreamland

Last night I had a dream
About a magic land full of magic

I was excited
Enjoying wands waving everywhere
Rabbits bouncing here or there

Suddenly a red dragon flew past
Roar! went the dragon loudly
As the sun smiled on him

All of a sudden I was awake
My puppy was licking my face
I was happy.

Bobby Blake (8)
Bysing Wood Primary School, Faversham

The Jungle

Once upon a dream,
I was in a jungle
With my friends
And there was a small gorilla
Who seemed to be
Wearing trousers.

The jungle had many leaves
Covering the trees
They were swaying in the breeze.
The sky was pale like paper.

The gorilla thumped his chest
And roared like crazy
And ran at us madly
Then everything disappeared and
Evie shook me and woke me.

Dylan Morris (8)
Bysing Wood Primary School, Faversham

Dragons

Last night, I had a dream.
I found myself at the park on the swing.
There was a baby dragon.

The dragon is naughty, like a pixie.
The dragon roars loudly.
At night and in the morning,
The dragon is like a red apple.

Suddenly I feel a gentle shake.
It is my mummy, waking me up.

Holly Barker (7)
Bysing Wood Primary School, Faversham

Trains

I dreamed a dream.
I found myself on the train bridge.
The train went *whoosh!*
The high-speed train went as fast as a racing car.
I felt sad because I wanted to be on the train.
Then suddenly, I heard Mummy say my name.
It was time to wake up.

Hadrian Bharke (8)
Bysing Wood Primary School, Faversham

The Shining World

I dreamed a dream last night,
I was in the magical clouds,
I was running on the clouds,
I was sleeping on the clouds,
I looked up and saw stars,
They shone in my eyes,
They looked into my eyes,
They made me feel bright.

Effie-Anne Dean (7)
Bysing Wood Primary School, Faversham

Swimming Escape!

S wimming in the ocean, what did I see?
W hy it's sea animals, all staring at me!
I swam around with them, happy as can be,
M oments passed before I realised a shark was behind
me!
M e and the animals swam for our lives,
I didn't want to be eaten, so I found a spot to hide,
N ow as I was looking, ink was what the octopi shot,
G one was the fiercest animal, and my goldfish
danced like a robot!

E veryone was happy and went out to play,
S o we had fun all day!
C olourful was the ocean blue,
A mazing. Why? I haven't a clue!
P layful was the whole day,
E qually fun along the way.

Daniel Minani (9)
Fox Hill Primary School, Sheffield

Paddington And Me

P eru is where Paddington lives, sadly alone

A t 12 o'clock I have my lunch

D ad says, "How was brunch?"

D elish,

I say it was!

N ow it's 1 o'clock Paddington is stuck in a bin

G ood, I need to go help him.

T o be honest, I have never seen a more extraordinary bear

O n a boat, we go to England

N ever ever has Paddington seen a human.

A nd marmalade on toast is good.

N ever ever have I tasted marmalade.

D ad asks, "How is Paddington doing?"

M armalade makes a good snack.

E ngland has a stack.

Aiden Gowler (8)
Fox Hill Primary School, Sheffield

The Nightmare

The night before I had a dream,
It was definitely not good.
Deaf, blind, couldn't speak
Lost in an endless hole, very deep.
I'd yell into a room, a room I'd never seen
It was a full moon and on the weary, dusty window
Sat a big, black raven watching me.

The room was bare, it had nothing but a bed, a
wardrobe and a blob of blood
Smudged on the wall.
I'd looked away from the bird and looked back
To see it wasn't there anymore.
I ran out of the now-open door to walk into my
bedroom,
When I tried going back into the room, the door wasn't
there anymore.
Darkness consumed me.

Tanishka Harshan (10)
Fox Hill Primary School, Sheffield

Toothless

T he dark sky in the night-time... A dragon stands by

"O oh," said the ninja, "you can do a handstand." Wolf said, "Yes."

"O oh, look guys, there is a cave, let's go there!"

"T oothless, do you want to go?" "Yes!"

H ungry Toothless and Wolf and Ninja and me went to the cave.

"L ook guys, look, there are scratch marks on the wall."

"E ek," said Ninja in shock. "There's a black panther."

S trong Animal Land is where they live

S ecrets lie beneath the land.

Alice Blanksby (9)
Fox Hill Primary School, Sheffield

The Little Black Cat

There once was a cat who sat here,
Give it a treat, it will reappear,
I only see this cat once a year,
When I see her I give a cheer,
Hoping I'll see her crystal blue eyes,
Lighting up like stars,
Brighter than the night sky,
Her coal-black fur as soft as a cloud,
Hearing her sweet meow,
Taking a walk down the street,
Hearing her little padding feet,
Her small rosy nose twitching as she sniffs out her prey,
Don't forget to say hooray!
Hope I see this cat next year,
I hope that it will reappear.

Phoebe Poulton (11) & Katie-Jo Myers
Fox Hill Primary School, Sheffield

If There Are No Stars In The Sky

If there are no stars in the sky
How would you find your way home?

Sitting on a dock, by the sea
Stars fade away

If there are no stars in the sky
What would you play with in the night?

Ooh, oh, I forgot
I have a power beyond others

If there are no stars in the sky
The moon has no companion

I come here every night
My cat and I

If there are no stars
What do you have?

If there are no stars in the sky
Your life is over

If there are no stars in the sky
How do you see your family members that died?

Trisha Eboigbe (9)
Fox Hill Primary School, Sheffield

Nightmares

N othing will scare me, not even what I see.

I am as nervous as I can possibly be.

G onna have a nightmare tonight

H oping this doesn't turn into a fight.

T rying to forget about it

M ight stay in my mind for a bit.

A m I being pranked, or even tricked?

R ight, I'm determined to forget about it and that's what I've picked.

E ventually, I start to think with my hand on my head.

S uddenly I wake up to find that I'm safe at home in bed.

Ranae Abbott (10)

Fox Hill Primary School, Sheffield

Every Dream Is Not Good

I close my eyes and open my eyes.
I am in a different place,
A place with flying lions, pandas, singing birds and
unicorns,
Bamboo, green grass and blue rivers.

Last night, my dream was a nightmare;
Dead unicorns, dead birds and dead pandas.
The blue river turned to lava.
There was no grass
And the bamboo turned to endless fire.

There was a wizard who changed everything for two
years.
Now I don't dream...
Every year, I'm waiting.
Maybe next year, or maybe never?!

Amin Omer (11)
Fox Hill Primary School, Sheffield

Space

When I was young I had a wish
That I would work up in space on a satellite dish
Surrounded by the stars so bright
Down on Earth, they twinkled throughout the night

Floating around like a big balloon
I'd do my work in the light of the moon.
Huh, what's happening? It's all fading away
Then my mom says, "Wake up, it's Thursday!"

Luke Manning (9)
Fox Hill Primary School, Sheffield

All I Wish For...

All I wish for is to fly,
So I can see the stars nearby,
So I greet them and see them play,
I could stay up here all day!

All I wish for is to go to space.
I'd take my phone to see my face,
I can go to the moon, Mars and more,
And explore planets no one has before.

Then I make up a wish that my dreams could be true.

Alfie Walker (10)
Fox Hill Primary School, Sheffield

The Moon

T onight the moon is glowing bright
H igh waves crash against the rocks in the moonlight
E ight shiny stars connect in the sky

M any glowing stars you will find in the sky
O verhead the moon glistens in the sky
O ne grey dot looks different each night
N obody knows what it is.

Olivia Naylor (8)

Fox Hill Primary School, Sheffield

Football

F ootball really is the best,

O h, the ball hit my nose, oh no my back.

O h, again and again,

T he football teams I play for are Sheffield Wednesday and Sheffield United.

B last the ball, ugh you missed!

A ll you do is keep on missing!

L iverpool FC.

L ucky shot!

Nathan Taylor (8)
Fox Hill Primary School, Sheffield

Dragon

D eep in the cave are dragons
R oaring and growling are dragons
A ll the dragons can be dangerous
"G o, everyone, there are dragons!"
O n the mountains are dragons!
N ow the fire has begun.

Sonia Hussain (7)

Fox Hill Primary School, Sheffield

The Ocean

O ne day in the summer
C rashing on the rocks
E ndless waves rushing to and fro
A cross the deep blue ocean, dolphins swim
N ow the ocean is silent as night.

Sienna Gibbon (9)
Fox Hill Primary School, Sheffield

The Pyjamaed Lawyer Of Dreamland Court

In my sleep, I dream a dream of who I will be,
I will stand up tall and loudly call,
That I'm a Pyjamaed Lawyer in Dreamland Court.
And I will help one and all.

Case number one, Tiddle vs Bruto,
Tiddle the cat and Bruto the dog can't agree on their cake for the party,
Tiddle wants vanilla sponge while Bruto wants chocolate log.
And I will say, "Have one of each!"

Case number two, Tinker Bell vs Bob.
Tinker Bell the fairy is in tears,
Bob the beaver is chomping the magical trees, to make home for free.
And I will say, "Why don't you make a hotel made of candy called the Fairy Lodge?
For fairies and beavers in the whole world."

Case number three, Jasmine vs Emerald
Jasmine the alicorn has lost her brush,
To comb her knots from her mane,

Emerald the unicorn won't share her brush.
And I will say, "To share is to care so both can have happy manes."

My day in Dreamland Court is now done,
Now I'm going to Bruto's and Tiddle's party at the Fairy Lodge to have some fun,
With a funky hairdo by Emerald and Jasmine.

Alessia Cattanach (8)
John Rankin Junior School, Newbury

Night Fright

Once upon a time, I was having a dream
It turned into a nightmare and I started to scream.

I looked straight ahead, there were spiders on the wall,
I looked under the bed and snakes started to crawl.

As I tried to walk on there were puddles of blood
They were thick and gooey just like mud.

As I walked further on past tombs in the graveyard
This certainly doesn't feel like my granny's rose
courtyard.

Lifeless slow creatures, green, it's a zombie,
I tried to escape but the ground became swampy.

Amongst the duckweeds and reeds, like a maze, I was
lost
As the night got darker and colder I shivered in frost.

Bats and vampires circled around my head,
I feared they would bite,
Oh when will I awake from this awful fright?

Suddenly I looked for where I could go
But I felt like I was panicking, no signs, no roads.

I thought I was all alone
No people, no home.

I don't know but I think I'm losing sight
But suddenly I woke up,
Phew, there's daylight.

Bella Collins (10)
John Rankin Junior School, Newbury

Once Upon A Dream

Once upon a dream...
With a shooting star so bright
Let's start this poem with me
Because this is my poem, right?
In my dream, I think it's right
A dream that leads me somewhere bright.
Open that door with a big smile on your face,
You're in my world in a very different place.
Close your eyes and think of anything
And what you're thinking is what I'm dreaming.
In that dream, it looks amazing, with magic everywhere
And a cute bear sleeping.
But then things turn the wrong way,
Look around, look down to the ground,
It's cracking with a frown.
Clouds surround you like a bleeding red dart,
Kids are screaming to hell
So run away and wake up from that dream
And call for help.
What's that in the bushes?
It looks like a head...
Your day will be over in a count of three
Let's all count together... One, two, three...

Dominika Racz (10)
John Rankin Junior School, Newbury

Dreaming With Open Eyes

There was sand all around me, I was falling down,
Then suddenly I landed in the middle of a town.
There were boxes and brushes lying on the ground,
With people stepping out of vans and hurrying around.
Most of them were heading towards a large pit,
Some without and some with a specialist kit.
But when I arrived there, and what I saw,
Was more fascinating than anything before.
It was as big as two elephants, with razor-sharp teeth,
With claws as long as rulers on the edges of its feet.
Its face was fixed in a permanent scowl,
As though looking at something terribly foul.
It was complete, it was perfect, about to go in a cast,
It was a beautiful specimen of a distant past.
They were all archaeologists, triumphant in a team,
And there lay a magnificent dinosaur, the same one
from my dream!

Bhuvi Deegwal (10)
John Rankin Junior School, Newbury

Dancing Pirates

I see a ship
In the water
It is bigger than I 'thoughta',
It looks like a pirate ship!
I hop on board,
To see a thing I can never unsee,
'Cause I've got to be...
A dancing pirate!
I join along with the crew,
I bet you wish this was you,
I would love to sail across the ocean,
'Cause... I am a pirate too!
It is getting late,
I need to get to that gate,
But still the dance will keep going on,
Even if I am gone,
I bash my head,
And fall back in bed,
And remember everything I saw,
But my mind began a voodoo 'cause,
I saw them all in a tutu.
Then I look under my bed,

And something licks my head,
I fall off my bed,
I am dead!

Harrow (9)
John Rankin Junior School, Newbury

Where Dreams Will Be

They creep through your window in the night,
Some are joyful and full of delight,
While others tap into your worst fears,
Things that have haunted you over the years.

Flying through meadows of beautiful flowers,
Or being a superhero with super cool powers,
Some are wonderful and some are scary,
Dreams filled with monsters and things that are hairy.

But it's hard to be scared when you're all wrapped up,
All wrapped up like a baby pup,
And as you drift off back to sleep,
Your favourite dreams begin to creep.

They creep back into your head,
While you're snuggled up in your bed,
And this is when you will see,
That is where they'll always be.

Lily Johnson (10)
John Rankin Junior School, Newbury

My Feather Winged Friend

I met a dragon once in a dream,
She wasn't as scary as it may seem.
She was pink with big blue eyes,
But she had feathers on her wings,
Hundreds on each side.

I found it strange but also unique,
Her horns were rustic, curved and sleek.
Circles, swirls, moons and stars,
Her magic as bright as Saturn and Mars.

She lives upon the Lavender Hills.
She gets there quick with her flying skills.
She comes alive when I close my eyes,
Riding her back, soaring the skies.

If you don't believe me, yes, it's true!
And when you sleep, you'll dream of her too.

Lily Everett (8)
John Rankin Junior School, Newbury

Dream Big Dreams

D ragons, monsters, whatever you like,
R emember dream big! You'll be alright.
E arly in the morning we all wake up,
A bout our dream, we think how amazing it was.
M ake it up however you like.

B ig, big dreams are always the best,
I f you put your luck to the test,
G o for it, go! Start now, start!

D on't give up, no matter what
R ewrite the stars, your fate's as small as a dot!
E asy peasy it will be
A mazing it is you see!
M ake it up, wherever you go!
S o, go on then, go!

Phoebe Avarne (9)

John Rankin Junior School, Newbury

The Mystery Dream

One night, a girl went to sleep
She didn't peep,
Although it was Christmas Eve,
Because she didn't believe,
In her dream, she was in a castle,
No ordinary one, there were owls carrying parcels!
Inside were people with wands,
I forgot to say, there were uncolourful ponds,
She was there,
But she didn't care!
She heard a rustle,
But didn't pull a muscle,
So she opened her eyes,
And heard a bye!
But she heard a bell ring,
Then a morning sing,
Then she realised, she was in a dream,
Then there was a scream,
So she went to explore,
With a roar!

Edith Powell (9)
John Rankin Junior School, Newbury

A Dream, A Dream

A dream, a dream, once upon a dream,
As I drifted off,
My bed lifted off,
A dream, a dream, once upon a dream.

A dream, a dream, once upon a dream,
As the world was spinning,
I felt like I was winning,
A dream, a dream, once upon a dream.

A dream, a dream, once upon a dream,
I woke up in a magical place,
As luck would have it I always wanted to visit space,
A dream, a dream, once upon a dream.

A dream, a dream, once upon a dream,
Flying horses, wizards and Mary the fairy,
It was fantastic, not a little bit scary,
A dream, a dream, once upon a dream.

Imogen Lewis (10)
John Rankin Junior School, Newbury

Dream

Once upon a dream...
You're in my dream
Now let's wander in my world
Through the forest, through the leaves
Come and see the adventure I have planned for you
Up, up over the hill you see everything, slide down the hill. Weee!

Go through the forest, follow the path
Look where the path takes you
In the distance, you see the end of the rainbow
Under the rainbow
There! A unicorn

Then, out of nowhere, the world starts to spin
Dropping me off into a different world
A world with a lava floor
A world with a volcano
An upside-down world...

Neysa Amoah (10)
John Rankin Junior School, Newbury

The Dreams I May See

I close my eyes to go to sleep,
What dreams may come I'm yet to see,
Will I find myself with wings to fly,
Or in horrid darkness where I might cry?
I hope to be with my fairy friends
So we can laugh and dance till nightfall ends,
The winds of dreams are a funny thing,
I never know what they may bring,
Though I wish to see my lands of love,
The monsters of my past could fall from above,
These are the times to face my fears,
Tell them straight that I will shed no tears,
Dreams make me strong, I know it is true,
If I believe it, then so shall you.

Evelynn Wallace (9)
John Rankin Junior School, Newbury

At The Bottom Of The Deep Blue Sea

I'm lost, there is no one but me,
Then I turn around and suddenly see,
The deep blue ocean,
Waves hitting the sand in one smooth motion.

I run forwards into the ocean's warm embrace,
And see what I think is a dolphin race,
I swim a little further and I see a wonderful sight,
Everything seems so merry and bright,
It's like a splash of colour right before me,
It is a coral reef that before me I see.

I swim on and on,
But I stir and know it can't last long.
It was a dream, it wasn't real,
Yet it seemed so surreal.

Emily Stott (10)
John Rankin Junior School, Newbury

Just Dream

Every night, I roll into bed with tiredness and sink into my mattress.
My eyelids feel like heavy curtains and I can't stop falling.
An image appears in my mind and I slowly enter the image.

The images are random, it could be wizards, famous fairies, football, flying, dancing, pirates, etc, etc.
Dreams are night-time imagination.

Some dreams can cause nightmares, such as getting lost, losing your family, or falling off a cliff.
That's what dreams are.

Then after a dream *thump!* I fall out of bed ready to start the day.

Reuben Fairless (8)
John Rankin Junior School, Newbury

Float

As I start to drift off to bed,
Dreams start to flow to my head,
I start to float,
As if I'm on a boat,
I go high,
Way up in the sky,
Cherry the dog starts whining,
And I hear someone crying,
The stars stop shining,
And it is frightening!
A star!
How bizarre!
I ask why it's sad,
It says it's mad!
"I fell from the sky!
I don't know why!"
I tell her my name,
She said hers is Fame!
The sun starts to set and so she led,
Me straight to my cosy, warm bed!

Phoebe Davies (10)
John Rankin Junior School, Newbury

The Dream

In my dream every night,
I dream something very bright.
With a pretty creature,
A witch looks like a very nice picture.
I became friends with her.

I asked for her name,
"What's your name?" I asked.
"I'm Sofia," she said.
She was very hyper,
She was jumping and bumping into people.

It was night when we woke.
She told me everything.
"My mom and dad left me here when I was ten."
"I'll help you find them..."

Chloe Kaburu (8)
John Rankin Junior School, Newbury

Football!

Teddy was an eight-year-old boy who went to a
football game.
He first got outside of the stadium to watch
Manchester United vs Manchester City.
He went through security and found his seat to watch
the game.
When he sat down the footballer and the athletes
came out to play.
He watched till half-time and it was 2-2.
He ate some food and watched the second half.
Manchester City got an 89:59 and scored to make it
2-3 and won the game.
After he left all happy because he won the game.

Josh Brooks (9)
John Rankin Junior School, Newbury

The Cute Dream I See

I close my eyes to go to sleep,
What dreams may come I'm yet to see,
Will I dream of a butterfly's pattern,
Or a cute, little, fluffy kitten?
I hope to be with a friend I know,
We will run and play till the sun goes down,
The dream I have is all around.

These flowers I have make me smile,
This dreamland will go down in a while,
But I'm nervous and excited too,
So I quickly dream of something special,
And I love it so much, it comes true!

Mya Polehampton (8)
John Rankin Junior School, Newbury

The Milky Way

Once upon a dream,
Beautiful colours I see,
Stars are floating in the sky,
One by one, they pass me by,
Beautiful colours of the rainbow,
Just like outside my bedroom window,
Out of nowhere, I hear a sound,
Suddenly my heart starts to pound,
It's aliens everywhere!
Full of great love and care,
I had a little roam,
But then I realised it was time to go home!
I waved the aliens goodbye,
Then I disappeared in the deep blue sky!

Shanaya Gowda (8)
John Rankin Junior School, Newbury

Winter Wonderland's Sweet Castle!

In Winter Wonderland, there are spiderwebs as soft as silk,
There is fresh, new snow as white as milk,
A giant, massive, huge icicle,
You can't even break it with a jet-powered bicycle,
Now, now, what's this I see?
It's a massive castle, right in front of me,
It's made of sweets,
It's made of everything that's sweet, I just want to eat and eat,
Now I'm just going to take a bite,
And that will be the end for tonight.

Elise Horridge (8)
John Rankin Junior School, Newbury

Escape Your House!

I go to sleep in my bed,
I dream about what's in my head,
Then I see my house on fire,
I start to feel really drier,

Then I start to pack my stuff,
Before it burns into fluff,
I start to see the ashes and smoke,
Then I see a soppy bloke,

Then I see a heartbroken lady,
Carrying a crying little baby,
Then I see a painful boy,
Almost gone without joy,
Then I give him a hug,
But then we're out to run!

Arabella Breakspear (10)
John Rankin Junior School, Newbury

Help My Mother And Me

H elp me, please, I'm dying on my knees.

O h hello Mother, I'm very pleased...

R un for your life...

R un so far you reach the end of the world.

O h Mother, what have you done...?

R un, run, run...

N ightmare, help, please

O h, how I would die to be with my mother...

People be alerted about monsters
Let me go
Save me, please...

Erin Austin (8)

John Rankin Junior School, Newbury

Nightmares

N o one can find me
I n the middle of the night
G etting lost is the worst, especially at night
H iding under the stars all alone
T he moon is up high
M y heart is pounding, where am I?
A bandoned in the moonlight
R unning in the cold, frosty air
E asily frightened under the dark, starry sky
S uddenly, I'm back in bed, cosy and snuggly.

Aaria Pike (9)
John Rankin Junior School, Newbury

The Race

The day is done, I go to bed,
I open my eyes, I'm in a race.
I see ahead of me a racing track,
I hear around me the clapping of the crowd.
Now I start sprinting and rushing up the track!

Nearer and nearer I've nearly won,
As soon as I feel I've won, in a flash
A racer is there running and running,
We're neck and neck,
I see the finish line,
Then I realise it's only a dream.

Oscar Ruddock (9)
John Rankin Junior School, Newbury

A Walk Into Mystery

A walk down the path,
I'll have a laugh.
I see a new land,
Hopefully it won't be bland.

Dragons and green,
No one is mean.
Dinosaurs, unicorns,
With such great horns.
Fairies and magic,
Nothing is tragic.

Oh, this does seem
Much like a dream.
Yet I wish it wasn't so,
For I have no foe.
I just learned how to sow,
And so much more I know!

Hannah Goldschmidt (10)
John Rankin Junior School, Newbury

My Frosty Dream

In my dream, I sit at home,
It's made of ice, cool and white.
Aurora lights on a snowy dome,
Rainbow colours look so bright.

Playing my best Minecraft game,
Excited to be on a winning streak,
Dreaming of PVP battle fame,
An ultimate win is what I seek.

Curled up on my lap asleep
Is Blizzard, my pet Arctic fox,
With fluffy fur so deep,
He keeps me cosy to my socks.

Hari Sarajini-Hodge (10)
John Rankin Junior School, Newbury

The Wonders Of Space

As we look into the sky we see the wonders of space.
We go back to between 1950-1970
And we see the USA and Soviet Union race.
Then Neil Armstrong ends it all.
There are still things we left on the moon that look like a golf ball.
Stars are shining just like you
But there are still things to do
Like land a rocket on Mars.
As we get something out of a pocket of ours.

Zain Hussain (9)
John Rankin Junior School, Newbury

My Teacher Is Lost!

My teacher is lost, what will I do?
I'll need to figure it out soon.
Maybe an alien's got my teacher,
The pens and pencils, as well as her.
And they've captured my classmates, they are now in space,
It's now making my heart race.
What if they capture me too!
Oh, I don't know what I would do.
Although it may seem...
That this is all a dream.

Grace Hart (10)
John Rankin Junior School, Newbury

The Holiday

There I was, fast asleep,
Although I was asleep my dream had just begun.
I woke in a cabin.
I had an uncle,
He said, "Today we'll go on holiday!"
I squeaked and screamed, "Yay!"
I went on a bus... then I woke up.
I asked my mum, "Are we going on holiday today?"
Softly she said, "No."

Stan Bull (9)
John Rankin Junior School, Newbury

Lucky Duck

As I woke up
With all my luck,
In my dream I saw a duck.
When it went I followed it,
In my kit I was running fast.
Then I saw I had a cast
On my finger, I felt it at last.
I was running as fast as I could,
Until I couldn't, what would I do?
So I just sighed and I said, "Oh,
Now I need to go."

Nilesh Sharma (10)
John Rankin Junior School, Newbury

Giant Spider

In my dream I woke up,
Not in my soft bed with all my luck,
When I saw a fly,
It made me ask why,
Then my dream flipped,
As I felt something like a whip,
Then I turned around to see something looking at me,
It was a giant spider,
My eyes got wider,
Then I thought it must be,
Only just a dream.

Edie Osborne (9)
John Rankin Junior School, Newbury

Trapped In A Dream

I arrive. I am here,
I wish I was home. I wish I was near,
I look around to see what I can see,
A buzz, a flash, a bumblebee.
There must be life, it must be here,
I sense it coming, it must be near,
A hole is growing,
I really should be going,
I run, I shout,
But I can't get out!

Rose Creasey (9)
John Rankin Junior School, Newbury

Never Give Up

One day, one night,
I'm still standing,
I never stop going
Until I fall down,
I sing sadly forever,
But then I get back up again,
And keep going,
And never stop,
That is what you can do with
Your dreams and goals,
You are special the way you are.

Aoife Robertson (8)
John Rankin Junior School, Newbury

Me And The Space Dragon

Every night I dream,
I ride a dragon that is green.
View our whole galaxy,
As me and the space dragon fly.
We feel like it's time to wake up,
As we go through the stars and over the moon,
I wake up at noon.

And have a jam sandwich for lunch!

Fifi Douglas (9)
John Rankin Junior School, Newbury

My Theatre Future

F abulous fashion designs made to be

U nique as the eye can see

T otally awesome songs, let's hit the beat

U sher the crowds to their seat

R ecreate lives of many before

E xcellent moves hit the dance floor.

Esme Appleton (9)

John Rankin Junior School, Newbury

The Magic Wolf

The dark moon
There is a magic wolf
It's not just a wolf
It is a magic wolf
There is a magic wolf
And they look kind and happy
Wolves let me touch them and
They let me keep them and
Take them home with me.

Amelia Caplin-Bird (10)
John Rankin Junior School, Newbury

My Dream

When I sleep, my dream is a wonderful dream.
It's morning, I make sure my room is clean.
Before it could be seen.
I want to be a singer, just like Ariana Grande.
Her singing voice just blows me away.

Sally Kutesa (8)
John Rankin Junior School, Newbury

Me And My Dog

Last night I had a crazy dream
That me and my dog turned into fairies
And I got chosen to be a dancer fairy
So if you keep making your dreams great
Then you will be great too!

Eve Wheeler (9)
John Rankin Junior School, Newbury

In Ronaldo's World - My Football Dream

In fields of green where dreams ignite,
A football maestro, pure delight.
With every touch, the ball obeys,
In Ronaldo's dance, the game conveys
Through shadows of sleep, a vision clear,
Stadium whispers, a crowd to cheer.
Ronaldo's prowess, a dream's delight,
A dance with destiny in the soft moonlight.
His jersey gleaming, a beacon bright,
A dream where legends take this flight,
In the silence of night, a dream's trance,
Ronaldo's magic, a fleeting dance.

A selfie captured moments divine,
With my fantastic player, oh how they shine,
On the pitch of slumber, cheers across,
A snapshot frozen in sleep's embrace,
A cherished memory, time cannot escape.

Vivaan Bakku (8)
Kensington Avenue Primary School, Thornton Heath

Because Some Dreams Are Nightmares

The walls are dressed in rags of grey,
With boarded-up windows, just a glimpse of the sun's rays,
The curtains are mangled,
Like unkempt hair
Tangled and bleak, something from a nightmare.
A blanket of darkness covers the room,
I want to get up but I feel it's too soon,
But here it goes,
The air is so cold,
Snot running from my nose,
Goodness me, something runs across my toes!
I look to the left. There's someone on my chair,
When did they get there?
I slam my eyes shut and let out a scream,
Praying so hard for someone to save me!
Light floods the room,
"Honey, are you okay?"
Finally, my mummy came to save the day,
The walls are dressed in a pretty pink,
The window is bright, the sun shining in,

The curtains blow in the morning air,
They no longer look like tangled hair,
So glad the end is finally here,
But we must remember some dreams are nightmares.

Laila Sewell-Green (9)
Kensington Avenue Primary School, Thornton Heath

Trendy Designs

T rendy fashion is my thing

R ed to blue to purple to yellow, any design is possible

E legant ideas coming to life, flashing in front of my eyes

N othing can be better than seeing my own designs

D elhi to Paris to London, my designs are everywhere

Y es, this idea is amazing, bring it to life!

D resses, skirts, shirts and jeans, all of them come to my dream

E xtravagant designs blows everyone's minds

S ay yes to the dress!

I will guarantee to dazzle thee...

G lamorous fashion designer I will be

N othing can stop me from making my reality come true

S tart this wonderful journey with me.

Kaira Tailor (10)
Kensington Avenue Primary School, Thornton Heath

Last Second Goal

I dribbled past those who were in my way,
As if I was like Harry Kane.
My dreams were gonna come true this day,
Was I going to rise to fame?

It was me and the goalie, face-to-face,
Our dreams hanging on a thread,
By this same ball.
If I were to score it would be their downfall.

Adrenaline pumping through my veins,
I had to take the shot, I must.
To free myself from these shackles and chains,
That restricted me from my last hope,
I couldn't embarrass myself in front of these folks.

However, with a single tap I woke,
Was it a win or was it a loss?
Curiosity came while my dream departed,
Into an everlasting dark pit.

Miguel Kusi (10)
Kensington Avenue Primary School, Thornton Heath

My Extreme Dream

I wake up drifting through the galaxy.
Where will I go?
Where will I land?
Will I find a person that will give me a hand?
Or will I find a beach and play in the sand?
Will I find a stop to an old, dull train?
Will I find a forest in the rain?
I feel my feet hit the ground.
I look up and down,
Then all around.
Am I going insane?
Or is this a world with giant candy canes?
A girl walks up to me and says her name is Olivia,
She says she comes from Bolivia.
"Do you want to go back to your other world?
Blink three times!" she says with a twirl.
Off I go!
Back to my home.
Was that a dream?
Because that was extreme!

Skylar Madden (8)
Kensington Avenue Primary School, Thornton Heath

Fashion Designer

F lashing lights as I walk down the catwalk
A ll the models in my sparkling clothes
S miling, seeing my creations come to life
H alt, paparazzi clicking cameras everywhere
I 'm on top of the world
O ne dress rocks them all
N ow see my designs shine.

D reaming of my designs, bringing them to life
E veryone wants a piece of my mind
S ay yes to the dress!
I nspirations exploding in my head like fireworks
G reat fashion designer I will be!
N ow follow me on this journey
E xtraordinary it will be
R un with me to the catwalk dream.

Esha Tailor (9)
Kensington Avenue Primary School, Thornton Heath

My Teenage Dream

Once upon a dream,
It was my birthday and I turned 13.
I planned a party,
Of course it was football-themed.
Under the stadium lights we play
With laughter and cheers
We all come together with joyous tears.

I wish we could always spend time together.
Yet this isn't real
They just stay indoors on their phones and chill.

They need your help so talk to them
Get them out of those chains
Let them have fun so they conquer their fears.

Free your time, build your team
Make it happen and let's believe in my teenage dream.

Nyle Rafiq (9)
Kensington Avenue Primary School, Thornton Heath

My Crazy Dream

Before I rest my eyes,
Underneath the twilight sky,
I take a breath
To let my imagination fly high.

I'm on a roller coaster of rapid dreams,
Filled with many screams.
Cotton candy filling the air,
Chocolate rain descending onto my skin.
Something weird touching my hair,
Everything starting to spin.

The Queen of Hearts comes with her cards,
The place swarming with her guards,
I run, I escape,
Into a place of the unknown.

I lie tired
In this crazy dream,
As I get what I desired...
A crazy dream.

Alvita Justice Ndidi (9)
Kensington Avenue Primary School, Thornton Heath

Joudari's Time To Shine

I stand on the field with my heart beating fast,
Anxiously waiting for the ball that my teammate needs
to pass.
So I make my run into space,
I beat the last defender with my outstanding pace.

I take my first touch and have the ball at my feet.
Should I pass it or should I shoot?
There's only the keeper to beat!

Mbappé and Ronaldo have been here before,
It's my time to shine and make the parents... roar!

"Siuuu! Joudari scored a goal!"

Aymen Joudari (10)
Kensington Avenue Primary School, Thornton Heath

Life Is Like A Dream

Life is like a dream that is as mysterious as it may
seem,
That can grow like a team,
Ain't that about a dream?
Life is like a dream because you want to know what it
means.
Life gets hot like steam,
Ain't that about a dream?
Life is like a dream.
You get scared, then you scream,
Ain't that about a dream?
Here's a question I would like you to answer...
How does life seem?
Then say, "Ain't that about a dream?"

Gracie Cook Wright (8)
Kensington Avenue Primary School, Thornton Heath

Work It Out

No one has prepared me, I'm almost there,
I take a step and take one again,
You love me or hate me I don't care,
I just know that I'm almost there,

Day by day,
Step by step,
You keep getting nervous, 'cause I'm almost there,
I take a deep breath and take one again,
Only two steps left and I'll be there-

Prancing left and right, all I see is smoke,
How did I get here?
I hope it's a joke!

Samim K (9)
Kensington Avenue Primary School, Thornton Heath

Candy Land

In a land, you don't need a fan
You can find a man with no hand.
It's a land.
No need of a man.
Look, there's a fan.
Candy Land,
No need for a man, there's candy!
There's a girl, Mandy.
Now there's Andy
Who is looking for candy.
This is very handy.
Where is my candy?
Why would you steal it, Mandy?
Give me my candy
Or I will tell Andy.

Azraa Roy (8)
Kensington Avenue Primary School, Thornton Heath

Imagination

Your imagination can make a creation
Make even a constellation of your coronation
You're royalty as long you are asleep
In your beautiful dream
As long as you close your eyes
Your imagination will take you.
They will take you through
Just look at me I want to be like you,
Just like you I want to go into the sky
And I don't want to stay nearby
I want to follow my dream.

Livia Silva Castro (9)
Kensington Avenue Primary School, Thornton Heath

Martin Luther King Jr

We need to be equal,
We need to share,
We need to be kind,
But others don't care.

Martin Luther King,
Was sent to jail,
But his biggest dream,
Was not to fail.

Black and white people
Should be together,
And we can be,
Friends forever.

We should all,
Be good to others,
And our parents,
And sisters and brothers!

Eesa Choudhry (9)
Kensington Avenue Primary School, Thornton Heath

What Is Your Dream?

My dream, my dream, what about you?
My dream is to be a model.
Models, models, models, I love models!
My next dream is to be a famous actress.
I have been promoted for a movie
And my family members and friends come into
The VIP seats to watch my movie.
My third dream is to be a great swimmer,
Just like a mermaid
And a mermaid in the aquarium.

Zahra Kellman (9)
Kensington Avenue Primary School, Thornton Heath

Above The Clouds

There were starry skies
Where secrets lie
Up, up there beyond the clouds
There is a mystery to be found
Us humans, the only thing we see from the sky
Are raindrops coming down as if they can fly.

Too far up is where the stars stay
However sometimes they explore far away
We have to avoid a space disaster
And fly faster!

Nita Surafel (8)
Kensington Avenue Primary School, Thornton Heath

Dream

Somewhere in the branches overhead a blackbird whistles.

I can make out a single light,
A single window and I think of witches.

Now that I am alone with the night falling and wet leaves on my face
I cannot quite remember how the story is supposed to end
But you have ended it for me
Leaving a track of crumbs to your bed.

Nur Khan (9)
Kensington Avenue Primary School, Thornton Heath

My Dream To Be Seen

I have a dream to be seen
No, no I don't want to be a bean
I said I want to be seen
Dancing with the rest
Oh please, don't shove my phone up your vest
Take a picture of me on the screen
So I can be seen
And post it on YouTube as your meme.

Faith Williams-Flemming (8)
Kensington Avenue Primary School, Thornton Heath

Monsters

M onsters are scary
O ne monster is kind
N o monster is kind except one
S weets are bad for monsters
T reat monsters kindly so they will treat you
E ither you be kind or they will be rude
R espect monsters.

Misri Patel (9)
Kensington Avenue Primary School, Thornton Heath

The Safe Up

Once in my dream,
Me and my classmates went to the United States
To see Mr Beast
To have a feast
One day, Mr Daw came
And bought us a door!
Then we saved money to buy a monkey
After, Mr Daw bought us a swan
That's a funny dream!

Mouna Bovell Nai (9)
Kensington Avenue Primary School, Thornton Heath

Tree

"Do not cut me!" cried the tree
"Because I make you rain-free in my cool shade.
You rest, eat my fruits that are best,
Take in my fresh smell,
Let me live my life well."

Makiba Amanuel (8)
Kensington Avenue Primary School, Thornton Heath

Dreaming In The Sky

I had a dream
I had a dream
It was a real thing
The sky was yellow
But very mellow
I was flying in the sky
And it was very high
Someone said it was a lie
Then I sigh.

Kelly Wallace (9)
Kensington Avenue Primary School, Thornton Heath

Night-Time Wonderland

When you wake up in the morning,
You try to remember all,
The dreams you had last night in bed,
And when you do, they come in a roll!

First, you're in a spaceship,
Soaring through the stars,
Finding funky planets,
And meeting aliens from afar!

Then you find yourself back on Earth,
And in a racing car,
You pass third, second and then first,
Now you're in front by far!

After that you're an explorer,
Trekking through the leaves,
Across the jungle, forest and Arctic too,
You can go anywhere if you believe.

Now you're a time traveller,
Exploring ages long past,
Ancient castles and futuristic cities,
A journey in which time runs fast.

As the night-time wonderland unfolds,
And your dreams will gently sway,
Remember these moments of happiness and joy,
For in dreams, you'll always find your way.

Dima Mandziuk (11)
Llandrillo Yn Rhos Primary School, Rhos On Sea

Cakes And Cookies

C an my dream of a bakery come true?
A bakery for me and cakes for you.
K inder cheesecakes and brownies galore,
E veryone who enters will be begging for more.
S erving my customers with a smile on my face,

A da's bakery will be such a great place.
N utella cookies and cupcakes too,
D own the streets, there will be a massive queue.

C racking eggs and measuring flour,
O rders will come in a million times an hour.
O nly the best for my customers will do,
K eeping everyone happy will make me happy too.
I can't wait for my dream to become real,
E ven I can't explain how happy I would feel.
S o never give up or your dreams won't come true, if I can do it, so can you!

Ada Williams (10)
Llandrillo Yn Rhos Primary School, Rhos On Sea

My Family's Pet Bird

I love my pet bird very dearly,
But I have a theory
Why is he so chubby when he sleeps?
He chirps all day with so little to say at night
He always brings an excite!

He takes flight
Even at the peak of night
Well, that's before he gets to sleep.
His appetite is almost as bad as my brother's appetite!
He flings his food everywhere;
With barely any care
My family must bear
Charging the vacuum's battery a lot!

I can't think of anything to do with my time
Than to draw and write about my little budgie!
My mum let him take flight in our lounge
After that mad half-hour, we found bird poop on the
windowsill!
Now you know a little about my bird
And you know my theory... they never rest!

Georgina Hagley (10)
Llandrillo Yn Rhos Primary School, Rhos On Sea

Friendship Forever

Friendship is flying through the brightest of skies.
No one can hurt us, even with lies.
We saw a silver lining in every dark cloud,
Helping our friends made us so proud.
Whether we are on the ground, ocean or sky,
Forever friends as time passes by.

A dynamic duo, my best friend and I.
We jam to Harry Styles and reach for the sky!
We feast on caviar, we're living our dream,
Exploring new beaches and places that gleam.

Like Ant and Dec, we spend our time together.
We don't fight or argue, well almost never.
We dress the same and have similar likes,
From dawn to dusk, we ride our bikes.

We're two peas in a pod, from east to west.
My friend and I are simply the best!

Hana Carroll (10)
Llandrillo Yn Rhos Primary School, Rhos On Sea

The Land Beyond

Do you want to know how to enter the land beyond?
Maybe diving through a pond or using a wand?
Maybe it's not your time to go,
Nor your opportunity to know.
Maybe the land does not want to show...
Are you ready to go on an opportunity of a lifetime?
Well sorry, my friend, you can only go at night-time,
With the glistening stars to help you on your way,
And by the time you get there, it will be day.
You see fields of neon-coloured flowers as tall as
towers.
The sky is so clear here.
As you are just about to leave,
You take one final look at the trees.
You go through the portal, and there, you realise,
You have arrived back,
Because you see the mortals.

Ambar Sureya Jones (10)
Llandrillo Yn Rhos Primary School, Rhos On Sea

I Once Had A Superpower!

S uperpowers are the best

U p we go far from the west

P lace up, place down and around the place

E verywhere we go, night or day no matter whenever we go, we know we are still ace

R ound up, round up to see me fly, no matter when, you'll see me nearby

P ack it in now, I know you like it, just calm down and watch me galore

O nce in a while, it will happen, now and then be patient and it will happen a lot more

W ait now, hang on, it's here, the beautiful powers you dreamt away

E very day you have fun and play

R oam about the world and dream away

S uperpower away, it went sadly, not there today.

Daisy Temple (7)
Llandrillo Yn Rhos Primary School, Rhos On Sea

Fantasy Land

F antasy Land is all about mythical creatures
A nd how they look with all their unique features
N evertheless, they all look so different and beautiful
T here they all are, looking so suitable
A s they stand nicely, ready to greet you
S ay "Hello" to not one dragon but two
Y ou find out that they are rare magenta dragons

L iving and travelling around in their special wagons
A lways happy to meet new friends, where
N ight-time has so much magic in the air
D on't worry, everything they do is done with care.

Madison Temple (9)
Llandrillo Yn Rhos Primary School, Rhos On Sea

Hey Teacher!

I know you think I'm a brick in the wall,
Scruffy, cheeky, running in the hall.
But you don't see the dreams I see,
Hiding deep inside of me.

The crowds that scream when I'm on the stage,
The readers waiting for me to write the next page.
The skyscraper that I will one day build,
The composer who likes their music chilled.

The oceans I'll cross and the mountains I'll climb,
The family I'll love till the end of time.
These are my dreams, so never forget,
You ain't seen nothing like me yet!

Grace Bowden (10)
Llandrillo Yn Rhos Primary School, Rhos On Sea

A Wild Cat

A place far, far from home,
A place where I wandered all alone.

The big forest was dark and deep,
And I had no idea I was asleep.

Paws stomping on the floor,
To the point I felt human no more.

The grass on the floor smelt better than ever,
But sadly, this dream wouldn't last forever.

Cats surrounding me left and right,
But then I woke up in a fright.

Seren Evans (11)
Llandrillo Yn Rhos Primary School, Rhos On Sea

Dreamland

Close your eyes and fall asleep,
Walk into your dream through the fairies' keep.
A world where only you belong,
Enter this realm with a whispered song.
A universe you manifest,
That comes alive when you rest.
Creatures imagined, big and small,
Fairies care for one and all.
Crystal clear waters and the trees lush green,
The most exquisite land you will have ever seen.

Georgie Naylor (8)
Llandrillo Yn Rhos Primary School, Rhos On Sea

Untitled

At night I sleep and dream of adventures,
Of monsters and beasts,
Then finish my quest,
With trophies and feasts.

Fireworks go pop,
Like a minotaur's head,
When I swing my sword
And chop him down dead!

When I wake up and
Hear voices in my head
They say
You are a demi-god!

Ophelia McGuffie (8)
Llandrillo Yn Rhos Primary School, Rhos On Sea

Famous Dancer

F abulous dancer moves like a dream.

A lways so gentle, graceful and clean.

M aybe one day I could dance the same.

O h, so delightful, I'll tell you her name.

U rsula Garvey who specialises in jive.

S eeing her dance makes me feel so alive!

Caitlin Dean (8)

Llandrillo Yn Rhos Primary School, Rhos On Sea

Deadly Dinosaur

Once upon a dream
I was wandering through a forest in the dead of night
Looking for a dinosaur
On my left and right.

Suddenly the leaves began to rustle
And my heart stood still
Before me was a dinosaur
Ready for the kill.

Reece Gallagher (9)
Llandrillo Yn Rhos Primary School, Rhos On Sea

A Dream

Unicorn lover
Dragon flier
Animal creator
Colour experimenter
Food eater.

L Jones (9)
Llandrillo Yn Rhos Primary School, Rhos On Sea

Arsenal Experience Gone Wrong

Once upon a dream of mine,
My bones felt weird.
I was at the Emirates Stadium,
As a gold shape-shifter with a long beard!

The pitch somehow made me a famous character.
It was a hot day in North London's masterpiece
That can hold 9,000 people.
The sun was as hot as a metal seatbelt in summer.
Then... *Bam!*

The pitch collapsed with everyone inside.
My friends survived in VIP.
They didn't have to suffer the worst thing to imagine.
All of a sudden, I shape-shifted into all of my friends.

It was as ugly as a witch who was 158 years old.
I was as tall as a skyscraper
And as bouncy as a kangaroo.
Everyone ran away.
What an eventful day!

Jayden Corbett (8)
Milwards Primary School & Nursery, Harlow

Escape The Jungle

You will never believe
What a fantastic and freaky dream I had.
I went to bed...
Suddenly, I went into a very stinky green slide.
I found an ancient emerald.
Kabam!

In front of me was a jungle,
With loads of animals.
Deadly rattlesnakes, slithering around my feet,
Monkeys swinging across the trees onto the vines.
Everything was going to plan until now...

I fell down, down, down... I fell with a bang,
Into an escape room with two lions
Who were ready to eat meat.
I ignored it then I looked to the left.
I saw a big, fat gorilla roaming around.

I was starting to itch, on my neck were thirteen spiders.
I had to find a way out.
Over there was a key!
A door opened with a clown in front of it.

The spiders were on my side.
They jumped on him and he fell down.

The door opened and there it was... Freedom!

Harrison Blayney (7)
Milwards Primary School & Nursery, Harlow

The Dazzling Football Game

Once, I was sleeping in my magnificent bed
I woke up in the Emirates Stadium
It was as bright as the sun
The fans were cheering as loud as a rocket
They were about to play an amazing game
Suddenly, the referee shouted my name for a
substitute
So I took a shot
The ball smashed into the net, *boom!*
Everyone roared like a horn from a boat
I did the Ronaldo 'Siuuu' and everyone jumped on me
And then I woke up
And said to myself
"That was the best dream ever."

Noah Lewis (8)
Milwards Primary School & Nursery, Harlow

The Wizard School

I woke up in a wizard school,
Lots of people staring at me,
One of the students was called Hermione
Hermione is as kind as Miss Honey.
I went in my room,
I started floating,
I swung my arms while I was sleeping,
I started having a weird feeling about my pillow,
I woke up and saw a light,
I started to swing my arms towards the light,
I found out it was a secret stash of candy,
I realised my pillow was made of cotton candy,
For some reason, everyone was floating including me!

Areesha Qasim (8)
Milwards Primary School & Nursery, Harlow

A Dream Of Heaven

I woke up in a world of heaven,
Fairies were flying as slow as a snail.
Suddenly a unicorn said, "I will guide you."
Then I realised unicorns can talk!

She was as beautiful as a flower.
I love the brave, wonderful unicorn.
But then I heard a crash and a bang!
It was my sister, she said, "I found the way out."

So I went with her
I didn't want to go, but I had to
I said goodbye.
When I woke up I realised it was a dream.

Samirah Nasreen (8)
Milwards Primary School & Nursery, Harlow

Bad Lego Land

Once upon a dream, I woke up in the strangest world,
With my brother and dad.
My dad told me to run as fast as a cheetah.
He told me to run because there were bad people trying to kick,
As strong as a gorilla.
I couldn't find anything to fight back, so I just got a stick.
Suddenly, golden Lego rose up and boring houses went down.
A flying cheetah came down for me to ride.
I helped my brother and dad come up on my flying friend,
As fast as a rocket, we escaped!

Micah March (7)
Milwards Primary School & Nursery, Harlow

Hogwarts School

You find owls at your front door,
With letters in their long yellow beaks.
Everybody shouting downstairs,
Suddenly, the doorbell rings.
Owls keep throwing letters at you,
And your uncle is shouting curiously.
Hagrid comes to the door, saying,
"Harry, you have to come with me!"
So you go with Hagrid to the train station,
And meet these incredible people.
You walk through a wall as huge as a house,
This is the best dream ever.

Ella Findon (8)
Milwards Primary School & Nursery, Harlow

122

Once Upon A Dream

I woke up in a world of sausage dogs,
I had the ability to talk to animals.
A sausage dog said, "Hey! You! Where do you think
you're going now?"
The dog was as fast as a flash and running towards
me.
Darkness was all around me,
There was steaming fog all around me,
Everything was dark.
The sausage dogs were scared, so they wiggled
towards me.
Everywhere was covered in smoke,
I couldn't see a thing.

Vyara T (7)
Milwards Primary School & Nursery, Harlow

My Life As A Mermaid

I woke up in shock,
My friends and I were mermaids and I was on a rock.
It felt like the ocean sea,
We were all jumping with glee.
Ahh, all the water in the pool,
But we had to go to school!
The water was sinking, we would all fall apart.
It was starting to get dark,
It was as dark as a black hole,
It was so dark I swam into a pole.
Suddenly, I woke from my dream.
I guess not everything is as it seems.

Abigail Dockerill (8)
Milwards Primary School & Nursery, Harlow

Untitled

I woke up in a world with super strength,
I was flying to a pond,
Pirates flowing in a boat
Fish jumping as high as a dolphin,
I saw crocodiles in the whooshing sea,
I was so confused,
Pufferfish eating cookies,
I walked into a plane,
And went to USA,
The plane crashed but,
Safely we survived!
I woke up with pain but we were having fun!

Kajetan Woloch (7)
Milwards Primary School & Nursery, Harlow

I'm Stuck In A World Of Chocolate And Cake!

I woke up surrounded by cakes,
Then I saw chocolate flakes,
The cakes were as gigantic as a house,
Chocolate as small as a mouse,
Big fluffy cakes,
And small chocolate flakes,
Boom! A chocolate balloon explodes,
Chocolate is everywhere, loads and loads,
The cakes were as fluffy as a cloud,
But when I had a piece, it was really loud.

Amelia Taylor Cook (7)
Milwards Primary School & Nursery, Harlow

Once In My Brain

In my dreams every night, I wake up in a flying balloon.
I am with my friend Flip and my dog Maggie.
We spot a balloon house. Then a thunderstorm comes!
Boing! Boom! Smash!
We see a monster with green scales.
He is slimy and with teeth as sharp as a knife!
Roar! Grunt! What is that? I don't know.

Zachary William (7)
Milwards Primary School & Nursery, Harlow

The Magical Dream At Hogwarts

In my dreams every night I imagine I'm in Hogwarts
With people swishing by on brooms.

Witches making brews in the science room
A game of Quidditch is being played.

Wizards creating spells, *bang, crash, pow!*
Then I wake up and pinch myself.

What a magical dream!

Evie Yeomans (8)
Milwards Primary School & Nursery, Harlow

Once Upon A Prince

I was in the middle of nowhere.
People came to me.
I was scared.
They took me somewhere.
To the White House, which is as vast as a skyscraper.
I went in, someone showed me around.
There was a shop with sweets only.
The sweets tasted like coke.
Then I woke up.
What a crazy dream.

Riley Chingwara (7)
Milwards Primary School & Nursery, Harlow

Superheroes

I woke up in a world of superpowers.
I had super strength and could shoot out fire.
I could climb really fast like the Flash.
I saw other superheroes.
One could fly, the other one had super strength.
I saw Doctor Strange, he went in a portal to defeat the Ender dragon like a beast.

Noah Thompson (7)
Milwards Primary School & Nursery, Harlow

Angels

I woke up in a world of wonder.
I saw angels flying around singing beautiful songs
They gave me some grapes because I was the queen of
the angels
We played tag and I was the tagger
And I tagged one and my bed was a cloud
And I slowly woke up.

Lily Turkoglu (8)
Milwards Primary School & Nursery, Harlow

The Magic Cook Book

In my dreams every night,
I wake up in a cooking mood,
I stroll to the library,
And I find a cook book,
It starts to flash and shake,
Magic whizzes through me,
When I eat the delicious dessert,
What a scrumptious dream!

Elsie Thomas (8)
Milwards Primary School & Nursery, Harlow

Magic Dream

I woke up in a strange world
where I saw Harry Potter.
He was doing a spell on a fish
and it turned into a dragon.
It was as cute as a baby cat.
I saw thousands of them in a river nearby -
they were jumping out of the water!

Olivia Fick (8)
Milwards Primary School & Nursery, Harlow

The Dino Land

In my dreams are dinosaurs in a forest
The forest stretched forever to a castle
So I sprinted to it
But there were three dragons breathing fire
And roaring who came and knocked over trees.

Frankie Lee (7)
Milwards Primary School & Nursery, Harlow

Untitled

I woke up in a school of magic.
Wizards were floating around me,
Dashing in a world of danger.
Spells sizzling!
Bang! Fozz! Zoom!

Oliver Sutton (7)
Milwards Primary School & Nursery, Harlow